# THE LITTLE HISTORY OF
# BRITAIN

This edition published in 2016 by Prion Books
An imprint of the Carlton Publishing Group
20 Mortimer Street
London WIT 3JW

First published in 2006 as *The Reduced History of Britain*

A CIP catalogue record for this book is available from
the British Library

ISBN 978-1-85375-967-3

Printed in Dubai

# THE LITTLE HISTORY OF
# BRITAIN
## REVOLTING PEASANTS
## & ROPEY ROYALS

**CHAS NEWKEY-BURDEN**
ILLUSTRATIONS BY TONY HUSBAND

PRION

# Introduction

Britain, eh? Such a brilliant place to live, what with the greenness and pleasantness of our lands and all that. By our calculations, historical stuff has been happening on our pastures green for more than 7,000 years and what a tea-swilling, beard-singeing, happy-slapping time it's been.

Of course, we know what you're thinking: how could we possibly cram all the stories of heroism (and heroic failure) that helped to put the G in GB, into one book – especially a book as perfectly formed, but, let's face it, small, as this one? Luckily, dear reader, that was our problem, not yours. We have scoured parchments, newspapers and books by the truckload so you don't have to. Instead, sit back, relax and enjoy (very) abbreviated highlights from Britain's history craftily condensed into 101 moments of, um, momentousness. God save the Queen and all who sail in her!

# ONCE UPON A TIME...

# The original Farmer Giles

Hunter-gatherers become sower-reapers

"Oi! Get off me land!" It is quite literally possible that these were among the first words ever spoken in Britain. The Neolithic period (circa 5000 BC) saw the people of Britain evolve from hunter-gatherers into farmers. Those who had previously chased wildlife around for food now learned to sow and reap; rather than hunting animals, they learned to put them to work on their farms. This also meant that settled British villages began to become established for the first time – as hunters, the population had previously moved around in pursuit of their prey.

Clothing was fairly basic, though occasionally embroidered with ghoulish necklaces made out of dead animals' teeth (not unlike what angry teenage Goths wear now). Life expectancy was around 30 years in this age but the early Brits made the most of their time on earth and some of them built perhaps the most amazing monument in Britain's history...

# A monumental achievement

The construction of Stonehenge takes ages

We've all done stuff in our lives that we're especially proud of: coming second in an egg-and-spoon race, solving the numbers round on *Countdown* or making a particularly tasty club sandwich. But even these colossal achievements are put in the shade by the building of Stonehenge. Completed in 2300 BC, after 1,500 years of work and extended tea breaks, it's an awesome feat of construction that three different cultures – Windmill, First Wessex and the Beakers – played a part in.

Its purpose remains a mystery – theories include that it is a clock or a launching point for spaceships – but in recent times it has taken on spiritual significance for many. Nowadays, man, quite a few people enjoy, like, prancing around the mega-sized stones with flowers in their hair and curiously dazed expressions on their faces. Heavy!

# Bring the bling!

Brits coin it in for the first time

Nowadays, we all agree that coins are rubbish – they don't buy you much down the shops, they make your pockets sag and then they cause your washing machine to go on the blink when you forget to take them out of your pockets. But imagine the excitement in 150 BC when the first metal coins arrived in Britain! Before then, bartering had been the main currency of local markets so when metal coins arrived they quickly became symbols of wealth and class – the bling of the olden days, if you will (and you will).

From prized status symbols to unwanted lumps of metal that people dump into the hands of the homeless or charity collectors, don't you think the story of the British coin speaks volumes for how greedy we have all become? We're all guilty and should be thoroughly ashamed of ourselves…

# Hopalong Claudius

Limping Emperor hobbles to power

In 55 and 54 BC, Julius Caesar engaged in a bit of sabre-rattling when he twice invaded Britain but on both occasions fell short of actually conquering – content just to prove he could quite easily have done so. Any Brits who might have called him a big yellow chicken were laughing on the other side of their faces 11 years on when Emperor Claudius turned up. With four armies and a bunch of elephants in tow (nice touch), Claudius conquered Britain and in doing so swept aside any doubts that his limp and stammer made him in any way soft. It was a bit like the day at school when the weedy victim of the class bully suddenly hits back. Only on a national scale.

Emperor Claudius himself stayed in Britain for only 16 days but his men successfully made Britain part of the Roman Empire. This development united Britain and influenced our language, culture, architecture and so much more.

# Killer Queen

Angry tax-dodger Boudicca runs riot

We all fear that moment when the brown envelope from the Inland Revenue lands on our doormat demanding money because we know we are totally powerless in the face of the taxman. Or are we? When the Romans visited the recently bereaved Queen Boudicca to demand some taxes, she didn't just send them packing, she spent months chasing them around the country and destroyed major towns on her way. (To be fair, Boudicca almost certainly didn't owe the money they were demanding and the Romans did attack her and her two daughters during their visit.)

Boudicca led her tribe to Camulodunum and burned the temple, then they moved to London, which they burned to the ground, and on to St Albans which they also wasted. Go, girl! Legend has it that Boudicca and her daughters committed suicide and that the fiery Queen is now buried underneath platform 10 at London's King's Cross station.

# The great wall of Britain

Hadrian's heroic hurdle

It spanned 73 miles and took around six years to construct. No, we are not referring to comedian Jimmy Carr's big fat head, we're talking about Hadrian's Wall. In AD 122, the Roman Emperor Hadrian visited Britain and ordered the wall to be built in the north of England. After flicking through ye olde Yellow Pages and finding a few hundred reliable builders, work began on this remarkable wall. Opinions differ on why it was built. To separate Romans from the Barbarians? A customs frontier? A symbol of Roman power? Hadrian knew... but he's dead so we can't ask him.

# For God's sake

Christianity comes to Britain

When you come back from holiday, you might have some duty-free ciggies or presents from abroad in your suitcase. But imagine arriving on these shores with something far more profound in your luggage – Christianity itself! That's what St Augustine did in 597. He was sent by Pope Gregory to bring the Roman brand of Christianity to Saxon Britain for the first time and he quickly converted King Aethelbert and built a monastery at Canterbury.

Not that the job was complete: it wasn't until 1384 that theologian John Wyclif and his followers produced the first English-language bibles. And thank God that they did. Think how boring school would have been without those Religious Education lessons to liven things up.

# Horny invaders

Vikings impose "Danelaw" on most of Britain

Nowadays, tabloid newspapers are quick to warn the British public of alien threats — real or imagined — to our way of life. If only the red-tops had existed in 793, they'd have spotted those pesky Vikings a mile off! For that was the year that Viking pirates raided a Christian monastery in north-east England. Then, in 865 a "Great Army" of Danish Vikings invaded England and battles across the country ensued.

The Vikings conquered all of northern, central and eastern England — as well as parts of Scotland, Wales and the Isle of Man — and named the territory Danelaw. Political correctness gone mad, as the tabloids would have said. Only Wessex remained Anglo-Saxon and in 878, the Vikings attacked there, forcing King Alfred to flee. What happened next includes a tale of, um, exaggeration that suggests the tabloid spirit was alive and well in this era...

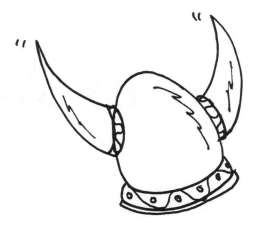

# His royal dryness

Alfie burns cakes to a cinder

"Who burnt all the cakes? Who burnt all the cakes? Big King Alfred, Big King Alfred – he burnt all the cakes!" That was a football chant popular on terraces throughout Britain during the 16th century. Okay, that's not actually true, but then neither is the story about King Alfred and the burning cakes strictly legit either. According to legend – legend here being ye olde English equivalent of spin – while a fugitive in Somerset marshes after the first Danish invasion, Alfred was offered shelter by a local peasant woman who was unaware of his identity. She asked him to keep an eye on some cakes she was baking.

Preoccupied with more pressing matters, Alfred let the cakes burn and was given a good roasting by the woman – though not of the Premiership footballer variety, of course. When she realised who her negligent guest was, she apologised. In reality, far from being a helpless and hapless fugitive at this time, Alfred was actually plotting his next move against the Vikings. The leader of England spinning a load of baloney at war-time? You'd never get away with that nowadays…

"Tut, I've told you before – 15 minutes at Gas Mark 4."

# Canute waves 'em off

Water way to make your point

Brown-nosers of the world beware: there is a limit to the amount of grovelling that the rich and powerful will accept. Take Danish King Canute, for example. He became the ruler of England in 1016 and made a rather fine job of it. The respect he earned overflowed into outright flattery from his courtiers and Canute grew tired of their words of insincere praise.

One day he was taking a stroll by the sea, surrounded by his grovelling men, and he decided to teach them a lesson. He asked them whether they thought he was so great that he would be able to stop the waves from rolling towards the shore. "Of course," they told him, apparently. "You're the most amazing guy, like, ever!" Needless to say, he didn't manage to hold back the waves and told his gushing courtiers that only God had the power to control the sea.

His reputation as a religious, God-fearing man was thus cemented. However, he did go on to commit bigamy and become implicated in a series of political murders. So perhaps his fear of God, not unlike his wave-controlling abilities, was somewhat overestimated.

"Keep on trying, Your Highness.
We're sure you'll stop the next one... "

# Edward confesses

He's gotta have faith

You're just dying to learn more about Edward the Confessor, aren't you? Well, you've come to the right place. King between 1042 and 1066, the pious Edward offended many by filling his courts with Norman friends he had made in Normandy (as you do). He had to face off a Saxon-led rebellion against him in 1052 by restoring some of them to their positions.

Perhaps the most visible legacy of his reign is Westminster Cathedral, a building he had built for the nation. All monarchs since then have been crowned there. A more immediate legacy, though, was the right bleeding mess the dithering King left behind by not resolving who would succeed him on the throne. There's nothing like a good old scrap and thanks to Edward's indecision, there was a huge one on the way...

# The eye has it

An arrowing time for Harold!

Christmas, eh? What a lovely day it is: loads of lovely grub to eat and all those presents to unwrap. In 1066, William The Conqueror had a particularly great Christmas Day: he was crowned King of England!

Following Edward's death, William and Harold had battled out their rival claims to the throne near Hastings. William's men were fresher and the English lost the battle, with Harold himself getting killed by a Norman arrow hitting him in the eye. His two brothers had also died earlier in the day. None of which set up a particularly fun festive season for the Harold clan — must have been a bit like those awful Christmases they seem to have every year in *EastEnders*…

# It makes census

William commissions the Domesday book

Some 19 Christmases on from his first as king, William the Conqueror hatched a plan to put together a record of who lived where and what they all owned. Notes were even taken of what livestock people had in their possession.

Historians disagree as to whether the survey was undertaken for tax purposes or to settle disputes over land rights. In all, it took 13,418 officials to conduct this ambitious census but only one person to write it all up - similar in many ways to the work behind the equally significant book you have in your hands right now.

# That's nailed it!

Edward hammers the Scots

You could be forgiven for thinking that medieval times saw nothing but a series of scraps as rival forces shed blood in their lustful search for power. So you'll be delighted to learn that when Edward I was asked to decide which applicant for the vacant post of King of Scotland to give the job to, he happily gave the nod to John de Balliol and they all lived happily ever after.

Only, they didn't. Balliol didn't turn out to be quite the stooge that Edward hoped he would be. Balliol decided to take sides with France – a country Edward was rather hoping to invade – and then started raiding England. Edward was furious and marched north to invite John to come and have a go if he thought he was hard enough. He hammered the Scots: more than 13,000 people were killed and Edward ordered that their rotting corpses be left in the streets as a warning to anyone else who might threaten him. Ewww, the smell.

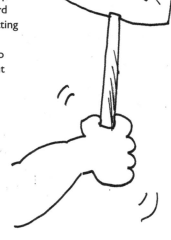

# The rebel yells

In common with nearly all bloodthirsty rebellions throughout history, the uprising of William Wallace began with an argument over fish. According to legend, Wallace – a patriotic Scot and firm believer in Scottish independence – got into a row with two English soldiers over some fish in a Lanark market place. He killed the two soldiers and his uprising was underway.

With fellow Scots joining him like a "swarm of bees", the man who became known as "Braveheart" murdered many Englishmen and then pulled off a stunning victory at the Battle of Stirling Bridge, where 5,000 Englishmen died despite the Scots being totally outnumbered. The following year he was defeated by Edward I and handed over to the English authorities, who emasculated, hanged, drew and quartered him before beheading him and placing his head on a pike on London Bridge. "It started with a fish," his head might have thought as it sat there, "never thought it would come to this."

# A web of deceit?

Robert the Bruce and the spider

Once upon a time, the King of Scotland lay in a cave. His troops had fought and lost six battles with the English and his family had been incarcerated. As he lay there on that miserable, rainy day, he was ready to give up hope entirely. Then he saw a spider try and fail to weave its web six times in succession. However, the brave arachnid then tried for a seventh time and succeeded.

And so it was that King Robert the Bruce was inspired to have one last go at driving the English out of Scotland – and he ultimately succeeded. What a lovely story, deserving to go alongside other memorably spiderish moments in history such as, erm, Spider Stacy playing the whistle (and beer tray) for The Pogues.

The only problem is that there is serious doubt that this ever happened. Historians now claim that the tale of the spider's web was, ahem, spun to take credit away from a powerful female supporter of Bruce who was really responsible for his inspiration. Sob, why do people lie?!

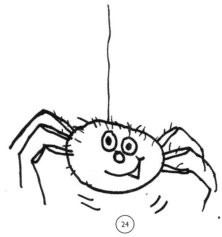

# The crusading King

Richard the Lionheart bunks off to the Holy Land

So much changes, so little changes. In 1189, a British leader went on a crusade in the Middle East – we've heard this once since, haven't we? However, courageous King Richard I, known as Richard the Lionheart, fought alongside King Philip II of France. Yes, you heard right! France! Fighting alongside England! In the Middle East! They captured Cyprus and Acre and then Philip went home to wait for Arsène Wenger to sign him for Arsenal.

However, on his journey home, Richard was imprisoned for a year by the German Emperor and was only released for £100,000. While his rival was in custody, Philip regained much of Normandy and Richard was to die trying to recapture it in 1199. His bowels were buried at the scene of his death… Sorry, what do you mean we've ruined your dinner?

# King John steals from the poor...

... and Robin Hood gives their money back again!

Now as we were all taught at school, if we all share and share alike, then everyone should be happy. But try telling King John that. You can't, because he died of dysentery hundreds of years ago, but even back when he was alive, he wouldn't have listened to you for a single moment.

A womaniser with a ferocious temper, he is believed to have murdered his nephew to secure himself easy passage to the throne. He was also a greedy sod. Once he had his backside on the throne, he hugely over-taxed his people to make up for the cost of fighting in France.

Where John robbed the poor to feed the rich, Robin Hood turned the tables when he and his band of outlaws robbed the rich to feed the poor 20 years later in Nottingham. Sound too good to be true? Well, there is no evidence that Robin Hood actually existed but he is still a hugely popular figure in British folklore, appearing in films, television shows and even computer games. So let's just all agree he was real and leave it at that. Okay?

# John brought to book?

The signing of the Magna Carta

In 1215, everyone seemed pretty cheesed off with King John - not least the barons who thought he had been taxing them far too heavily. Seeing trouble on the horizon, John agreed to the Magna Carta, which reined in his powers and subjected the British monarch to the law of the land for the first time. This was, however, just a stalling tactic for John and will, within three months, be reneging on his promises.

# The Black Death

Scary plague halves the population of Britain

In 1348 a ship arrived in a port in the south of England. Among its cargo was a plague that came to be known as the Black Death. Soon, the plague was spreading across the country and killing a shocking amount of people as it did so. Anyone who caught the plague would die within a week of first feeling unwell, often within a day or two.

Various theories were put about on how to stop the plague. Doctors noted that victims coughed up blood and decided this meant that they simply had too much blood and would extract blood from the victims. Which worked about as well as you would expect. Some people said it was a punishment from God and went around whipping themselves, others blamed and attacked Jewish people. None of which stopped the deaths, and between 1348 and 1350, up to 45 per cent of the population of Britain were killed by the Black Death, perhaps the worst disaster ever to hit Britain.

# Hate you long time

The Hundred Years War

Edward III had a dream: he wanted to become King of France. He had a claim through his mother but having a legit claim to a throne doesn't necessarily mean you get it. And so the Hundred Years War came to pass.

Despite being outnumbered and fighting on enemy territory, the English did well, thanks to good planning and their use of the longbow, a weapon not in the French armoury. The English won some glorious victories, including at the Battle of Crécy in 1346, but Edward was eventually forced to sign a peace treaty with the French, giving up his claim to their throne.

But then Henry V came to the throne over here and recommenced hostilities. Although he suffered some early humiliations, he won a crushing victory at Agincourt and returned in triumph after securing a promise that his son could become heir to the French throne. It didn't go quite to plan, though, and the English were eventually shooed away by baguette-wielding Joan of Arc and the King of France's son took the French throne.

Beaten. By a lady. A French lady. All said it was a bit of an embarrassment for the lads, eh?

# What a brawl!

## The Wars of the Roses

There's nothing quite like a battle over rival claims to the throne to really get everyone going and the Wars of the Roses made Leeds town centre at chucking out time on a Friday night seem tame in comparison. The Duke of York and the Lancastrian Henry VI both reckoned they deserved the top job and a series of scraps ensued.

The Duke of York thought he had won the first battle, but Henry's missus turned up and she wasn't the type to shout: "Leave it, 'e ain't worth it." Instead she simply beheaded her husband's rival. Then the Duke of York's son asked a few Lancastrians if they'd spilt his pint, won the next scrap and was crowned King.

By now, people from both camps were defecting to one another. Henry VI knocked Edward off the throne but then a few years later, the words "I'm back!" rang out and Edward returned to the throne. Everyone thought the scrap was over and headed off to queue at the kebab shop or to grab ye olde mini-cab home...

# Seconds out, round two!

The Battle of Bosworth Field

... But there was more to come! Edward reigned for 12 years and when he died, he assumed power would pass to his son – but the Duke of Gloucester had other ideas. He grabbed the throne and declared himself King Richard III. Was the fighting over? No chance! Now, Henry Tudor pitched up and said he was going to be king. Richard and Henry met at the Battle of Bosworth and asked each other: "What are you staring at?" Henry won the ensuing battle, became King Henry VII and the Tudor era was upon us.

"1–0 to the Lancaster..."

# Morris major!

Bet they looked bad on the dance floor

As you sit transfixed by yet another soap opera, desperate reality TV show or the 1,514,896th repeat of *One Foot in the Grave*, it is hard to imagine how anyone survived before the days of television. Just what did they do with their time? Easy. They dressed up in ridiculous costumes and pranced around waving handkerchiefs and sticks!

The origins of morris dancing are a contentious issue: some say it derived from pre-Christian fertility rites, others argue it came from late 15th century dance styles from France and Spain. Whatever, this colourful tradition quickly became a very British affair. Throughout the 1500s, it was performed at Easter and May Day and to coincide with the planting cycle as it was believed it would help crops grow if ale-swigging men jumped up and down on top of where they were planted.

Morris dancing was banned by Oliver Cromwell – see, he wasn't all bad – but restored by Charles II. There are still more than 14,000 morris dancers in the UK who regularly ponce about at village fetes. One Liberal Democrat peer even suggested that morris dancing should have formed a part of the London 2012 Olympic Games. In the name of sanity, no!

# Henry's wives

When one wife (or six of them) just isn't enough

That Henry VIII chap had more wives than you've had hot dinners. An exaggeration, of course: if that were true you'd be dead of hunger, or at least malnourished and bored. But Henry did go through a lot of ladies and kicked off with Katharine of Aragon. If your brother died, you'd be overcome with grief wouldn't you? But Henry VIII was such a charitable chap he managed to spare a thought for his brother's widow Katharine — indeed, he comforted her so much, he ended up marrying her. She presented him with a daughter, but then kept losing babies, so caring old Henry divorced her.

"I do, I do, I do, I do, I do and I do again…"

He had already had his head turned by Anne Boleyn and as soon as his divorce came through, he asked Anne "How ya doing?" and they married. She too only managed to produce a daughter and when she was accused of cheating, Henry had her beheaded.

He then went through four more wives, executing one of them along the way. Funnily enough, lots of other significant things happened during his reign, including the break with Rome, the union of England and Wales and the dissolution of the monasteries. But let's not remember him for any of that boring stuff. We want scandal and Henry gave us plenty!

# Golden Virginia

The life and chaste times of Elizabeth I

Her father had got married six times, but Elizabeth I will always be remembered as the virgin Queen. That doesn't mean she was part of Richard Branson's empire, because he blatantly hadn't even been born. Rather it meant that she never married.

There was enormous pressure on her to wed, particularly after she fell seriously ill with smallpox and Parliament ordered her to marry or name a successor to avoid a civil war upon her death. She still refused, so one can only conclude that men during the Golden Age must have minged big time. Not an allegation anyone could have thrown at Liz, who loved her sumptuous costumes and glamorous jewellery. She was also famed for having a very short temper. Think Sharon Osbourne of the olden days.

Her reign also saw a lot of conflict with France, Scotland, Spain and Ireland. England became a force on the seas, which helped subsequent colonisations. Indeed, Virginia, the first English colony in North America, was named after virgin Liz.

# Something to declare?

Raleigh discovers fags and potatoes

Nowadays, if a friend of yours went to America for their holidays and the only presents they brought you back were a jacket potato and a pack of Silk Cut, you'd feel pretty aggrieved. You might even harbour violent feelings towards them. But this was the olden days, the 1500s no less, and Sir Walter Raleigh went down in legend for his Stateside shopping trip.

A natural wit, Raleigh was a favourite of Queen Elizabeth I and legend has it that he once threw down his cloak so she did not have to walk through a puddle. After trips to the New World in the 1580s, Raleigh returned with tobacco and potatoes, which changed the face of commerce in Britain. Raleigh believed that smoking tobacco was a cure for coughing, and the Queen was so pleased with his contribution to the health of the nation that she knighted him!

Not all were so convinced by his tobacco haul though. A well-meaning servant, seeing Raleigh enjoying a pipe and believing he was on fire, threw a bucket of water over him. Worse was to come when Elizabeth's successor James I came to power and had Raleigh beheaded for treason in 1618. Raleigh apparently joked with his executioners and enjoyed one last smoke before the axe fell. From "roll your own" to "heads must roll", Raleigh's days of enjoying a relaxing fag (and breathing) were over.

37

# Ship ahoy!

Brits rob the Spaniards

In 1588, the Spanish finally got it together and sent the huge Spanish Armada towards Britain. The English managed to face them off at Plymouth and chased them away. They landed at Calais instead – probably looking to buy some cheap booze – and the English, inspired by the swashbuckling Sir Franny Drake (again), attacked the Armada using fire ships, sinking many Spanish boats.

As well as defeating the Armada, Drake had also stolen piles of bronze, silver and gold from the Spanish colonies. The Spanish argued that he was a pirate (they called him "El Draque" – the Dragon), not the privateer he claimed to be. But, hey, one man's thief is another man's opportunist. Let's rob!

# The Bard of Avon

Literary genius, big Willie-style

Dear reader, as you have pored through the witty and moving literary vignettes contained within these pages you may well have found cause to pause and say, "This is a positively Shakespearean effort." And we'd have to humbly agree.

Perhaps the greatest ever writer in the English language, William Shakespeare was born in Stratford-upon-Avon in 1564 and within a couple of decades was producing some of the finest plays ever written, including *Hamlet, Romeo and Juliet* and *Macbeth*. He was equally adept at penning (or should that be quilling?) tragedy and comedy and his plays remain monumentally popular around the world to this day.

Various spoilsports have suggested that it was not Shakespeare but someone else that was responsible for his work. But this is just jealousy, of a similar kind that the author of this work has had to endure for many years. There has also been speculation that Shakespeare – who dedicated much of his poetry to another man – might have been gay. What utter rot! A gay man working in theatre? We've never heard of anything so ridiculous!

"Romeo and Juliet? What sort of name is that for a play?"

# Nine-day queen!

The diary of Lady Jane Grey, the momentary monarch

JULY 10, 1553

Am staying at the New Inn in Gloucester.
Just found out I've been made Queen. Cool!

JULY 11, 1553
Have got myself a room at
the Tower Of London.
Hurrah and huzzah!

JULY 14, 1553
Oh balderdash! Apparently my succession as
Queen contravenes an Act of Parliament.

JULY 16, 1553
It seems that some woman
called Mary thinks she
should be Queen instead.

## JULY 18, 1553

All my staff have left the Tower, not sure where they've gone.

## JULY 19, 1553

My reign is over! Mary has been named Queen! All my staff went off to join her camp. V bad.

# Brits come together

The evolution of the British flag

England football fans have waved it in the faces of Scottish fans, even though it contains the flag of Scotland. When lead vocalist of The Smiths Morrissey paraded it on stage during a rock concert, people said he was racist, yet when Oasis did the same a few years later people said it was cool. Some councils have tried to ban it and in 2003 people tried to give it a makeover. Everyone calls it the Union Jack even though that isn't its correct name. Welcome to the strange world of the British flag!

The flag came about when James VI and I united the crowns of England and Scotland in 1606, merging the flags of the two countries. Later, in 1801, the cross of St Patrick of Ireland was added to give us the flag we use today. In recent years, the British have become more comfortable with the Union Flag and stopped assuming that anyone who so much as acknowledges it exists is automatically a nasty fascist bully.

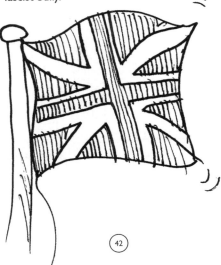

# Guy Fawkes rumbled!

Gunpowder plot blows up in his face

Al-Qaeda and modern anti-terror cops might think they're all hip and 21st century but they're actually so last year. In fact, they are so 17th century because religiously-motivated terrorists were plotting to blow up Parliament and the British police were using torture to draw information from them way back in 1605.

When James I seemed to renege on promises to chill out a bit with the anti-Catholic stuff, Robert Catesby decided to strike a blow for his faith. He assembled a team of plotters, including Guy Fawkes, and they planned to blow up Parliament. Sadly for the rotten scoundrels, word was somehow leaked to Lord Monteagle warning him not to attend Parliament on 5 November. The building was searched and Guy Fawkes was found in the cellar surrounded by gunpowder ready to blow it up. Erm, you're like so busted, Guy.

Meanwhile, his co-conspirators fled on horseback to the Midlands, where most of them were eventually tracked down and arrested or killed.

Ever since, Brits have marked Guy Fawkes night with bonfires and firework displays. Much more fun than the "War on terror", eh?

YE BIG BURNER

# Tea time

The great British cuppa arrives

As every British person knows, there is literally no problem, trauma or crisis life can throw at you that cannot be completely solved by simply drinking a nice cup of tea. The Chinese discovered tea 5,000 years ago but it wasn't until the 1600s that Brits caught on when Charles II's Portuguese wife Catherine De Braganza introduced us to the drink. Back then, a pound of tea cost the equivalent of a week's wages for most, but in the 18th century, tea taxes were removed and enjoying a good cuppa became an enduring tradition.

Each British person now knocks back an average of 2.5 kg of tea each year. Okay, so us Brits are a bit uncouth about the whole thing, adding milk and sugar rather than delicately flavouring it with lemon and gently sipping. But that's how we like it and to do otherwise just wouldn't... well, it just wouldn't be our cup of tea.

# The chosen one

King Charles thinks he's God's best mate

As we've seen, when Guy Fawkes tried to take on
Parliament he failed miserably. But Charles I was not the
sort of person who learns from the mistakes of others.
Arrogant and deluded, he believed he was God's chosen
one and this informed many of the bad decisions that
blighted his reign. The House of Commons got
increasingly cheesed off with Charles and he dissolved
Parliament for 11 years. He continued to squabble with
the Parliamentarians and when he tried to have five
members arrested that was the final straw for both
sides. It was war!

In Charles's corner were the Cavaliers, who were
drawn from the peasantry and nobility, in
Parliament's corner were the
Roundheads, who were dominated
by the emerging middle class.
Under Oliver Cromwell's
guidance, the Roundheads
defeated Charles's Cavaliers.
He was put on trial,
convicted of treason and
executed in 1649. No doubt
God was waiting in heaven
to give his saintly soldier a
special welcome.

# No ball games!

Cromwell bans everything that is fun

Nowadays, many politicians pretend to like football to get extra votes, but Oliver Cromwell decided to ban it when he came to power in 1653. A puritan to the core, he also banned theatre-going and closed loads of pubs. How to win friends and influence people, huh? He was even less popular in Ireland, where his followers slaughtered thousands in a bid to "tame" the Irish, who he believed were plotting with other Catholic nations to attack England.

After Cromwell died of malaria in 1658, his son Richard took over leadership of the country but made a bit of a mess of it and left the job in 1660. Charles II was then invited to return to the throne and the monarchy was restored. He quickly ordered Cromwell's body to be dug up and posthumously executed. Lovely.

# What a juicy pair!

Rogue Charlie gets his hands on Nell's oranges

That Charles II was a bit of a rogue, wasn't he? He boasted that he had 14 illegitimate children and went through mistresses at a rate of knots. He enjoyed a decadent social life and enjoyed nothing more than playing with his mistresses, surrounded by his pack of spaniel dogs. Perhaps his most famous fling was with Nell Gwyn, whose rags-to-riches CV read: prostitute, theatre orange-seller, actress, royal mistress.

A natural wit, Nell was always ready with a one-liner. As two men fought after one of them called her a whore, she shouted: "I am a whore, find something else to fight about!" Charles clearly enjoyed, ahem, plucking Gwyn's forbidden fruit – the pair had two sons together.

# Elephants on ice!

Londoners have brrrilliant fun on the Thames

Brrrrr, the winter of 1683/84 was a real shocker. Slap bang in the middle of a period in Europe known as "The Little Ice Age", Britain got so cold that fuel prices rocketed and much wildlife perished, including parks full of deer. Only one thing for it: let's have a party on the iced-up river Thames! Everything from bull-baiting to puppet shows and horse and carriage races went on as Londoners braved icy temperatures.

In previous years, Henry VIII is said to have travelled down the Thames on a sleigh for reasons known only to himself. Going back further still, in AD 923 a market was set up on the frozen Thames.

In 1814, the highlight of a "frost fair" was an elephant being led across the frozen river next to Blackfriars Bridge. However, by this stage the climate was growing milder and frost fairs were becoming increasingly precarious events. No sooner had they started than the ice would start melting, forcing everyone to run for their lives. Not all succeeded.

Some two centuries later, a whale was spotted swimming down the now unfrozen Thames one Friday. London's famously dedicated workforce immediately downed tools saying, "Sod this for a lark, let's go and see the whale!" And they all had a whale of a time... until it died.

# Feeling hot, hot, hot…

The Great Fire of London

Have you ever gone to bed at night and wondered whether you switched the oven off? Well, if Thomas Farrinor had done just that on September 2, 1666, the history of London may have been quite different. The baker, who lived in Pudding Lane, seemingly forgot to extinguish his oven and in the early hours of the morning, fire broke out in his home.

Most houses were built of wood and straw in those days so the fire quickly spread across London. It destroyed 13,200 houses, 87 churches including St Paul's Cathedral and made more than 65,000 people homeless. In many parts of the capital,

the ground was too hot to walk on for several days. Amazingly, the death toll is reckoned to be in single figures, though some historians dispute this.

Out of the ashes of the fire, a less flammable London emerged with buildings (especially bakeries) made from brick and stone.

# Let's get physical

Isaac Newton explains gravity…
but apple misses his head

Weren't science lessons at school
just the best laugh ever? All
those test tubes and explosions
and experiments. Jolly good
fun. Well, we have to take off
our hats to the father of modern
science Isaac Newton – without him, none of that might
have been possible. He was the sir of science, the father
of physics, the… [enough already, Ed.].

Newton's studies created much of the fundamental
understanding we have of the universe to this day. One
day, he saw an apple fall from a tree and realised that
gravity is a universal force. In due course, this story got
spun to suggest that the apple actually hit him on the head.
It didn't. He just saw it fall. People pretend that
the story is so much more fun than it actually was…
and why not, eh?

# Taking note

The Bank of England is founded

We've all silently fumed as banks shut their windows just as the queues get busy at lunchtime; well, the world of banking has always been a bit potty. In 1694, a Scotsman founded the Bank of England and a year later an Englishman founded the Bank of Scotland. Does life get any more crazy and hilarious? Probably.

Formed to be the government's banker and debt-manager, the Bank of England was first established to help bankroll the expensive wars of King William III. It also issued the first bank notes, which were originally individually hand-written; you can only imagine how much longer queues must have been during ye olde lunch breaks. At first, notes ranged in denominations of £20 to £1,000 but in 1797, the first £1 notes were issued and stayed in circulation until 1988, when they were replaced by a coin.

# The man who would be queen!

James II flees in a skirt!

Some people are just plain silly. James II was one of these people. England was strongly and proudly Protestant in the 17th century, but James thought it might be a nice idea to try and convert everyone to Catholicism. Bad move. As he promoted more and more Catholics to influential positions in public life, resentment against him grew. Fuming Protestant parliamentarians asked Dutch ruler Prince William of Orange if he would help them get rid of James. He said: "For sure" and very quickly, James donned women's clothes as a disguise and fled to France.

William took the throne. Since then, Britain has had a constitutional monarchy with the reigning monarch's powers limited in comparison to before. As for James, he tried to regain power in Ireland and Poland but lived out the final years of his life in France. Not wearing a dress though.

# Yanks, but no thanks

The Boston Tea Party and American independence

As we've already established, there is no problem at all that cannot be solved by a nice cup of tea. Ask the Yanks, they won independence by putting the kettle on! Okay, that's a simplification, but let's not run in fear of simplification. You see, the Boston Tea Party was the beginning of independence for America. Trouble had been brewing for a while but things came to the boil in December 1773, when a gang of Boston folk dressed up as Indian Mohawks and destroyed hundreds of crates of British tea at the harbour and threw them into the sea in protest at the British Stamp Act.

The British reaction to this stirred up more problems and sparked the American War of Independence. As this was a war that we lost, it is not a period of British history we need to detain ourselves with for long. We'd rather have a cuppa and forget all about it, okay?

# The workers bite back

The Tolpuddle Martyrs

Nowadays, if a bunch of workers knocked on their boss's door and said: "We want to be paid 10 shillings a week," he would bite their hands off in agreement. But this story is set in the olden days, the 1830s in fact. Six British labourers from Tolpuddle in Dorset were protesting against the lowering of wages and refused to work for less than 10 shillings a week. They formed a society and swore an oath to one another.

Big mistake. A local landowner wrote to the Prime Minister, pointing out that a 1797 law prohibited people from swearing oaths to one another. He's telling, he's smelling, he's going to Batman's wedding – but the six Tolpuddle Martyrs were going to Australia after being convicted of breaking that law. Their case received widespread support and they were released in 1836. Since then, they have become heroes to the Trade Union movement, which they are credited with inspiring. But if they think being sent Down Under was a bad punishment, they should have tried being in a Trade Union in Maggie Thatcher's days…

# Poetry emotion

William wanders lonely as a cloud

Nature, eh? Isn't it a beautiful and wonderful thing? It's enough to make a grown man break down and weep. Well, William Wordsworth certainly thought so. The poet who ushered in the English Romantic Movement, his work was heavily influenced by his love of nature and scenery. In 1843, he was made England's poet laureate and remained so until he died seven years later.

Willie was almost as good with words as the Arctic Monkeys. Perhaps his best-known poem is "Daffodils" a wonderful tale of the redemptive power of coming across a field of golden daffodils as he "wander'd lonely as a cloud". Sob, we're filling up here...

# Thrashing the French Pt 1

Nelson stands tall

"England expects that every man will do his duty": these were the words that Horatio Nelson used to inspire his troops before the Battle of Trafalgar in October 1805. For the past year, Napoleon had been plotting to invade Britain and Nelson was in charge of preventing this.

The key showdown came just off the Spanish coast at Trafalgar and Nelson guided his men to a famous victory. The combined might of the Spanish and French fleets were defeated without the gallant Brits losing a single ship.

"Good work, fella," people would have said to Nelson were it not for the fact that he was killed on his ship by a sniper's bullet during the battle. So instead, a square was built in the centre of London with a column-statue-thing in his honour as the centrepiece. It subsequently became a major attraction for tourists and pigeons alike.

# Thrashing the French Pt 2

Wellington's Waterloo walloping

More British pride was secured at the Battle of Waterloo – and plenty of it. They didn't just defeat Napoleon's men, they trounced them, killing at least 37,000 of them and bringing the reign of jumped-up short-arse Napoleon to a humiliating end.

This one-day battle took place in a small village south of Brussels. It was winner-takes-all stuff for Wellington and Napoleon and when the Wellington-friendly Prussians and Dutch turned up, the French ran for their lives. His spirit crushed, Napoleon subsequently surrendered to the British and was exiled to Saint Helena. Quel fromage!

# Penny post

Sir Rowland Hill achieves Parliamentary backing
for stamps

The world's first official adhesive postage stamp, the Penny
Black, was issued in Bath on May 1, 1840. It bore a photo
of the reigning monarch, Queen Victoria.

The modern postal service was officially in business.
Some people are still waiting in the queue that formed on
that first day.

"So I just need to wait for them to invent the post box."

# AND THERE'S MORE...

# Victoria's values

## The real Queen Vic

The in-depth research involved in writing this book has yielded a number of earth-shattering discoveries. For example: the Queen Vic pub in *EastEnders* was actually named after a real Queen! We know, staggering isn't it? But we promise that it's true.

She took the throne at the age of 18 in 1837 and reigned for 60 years – until Elizabeth II the longest of any British monarch. During her reign, the British Empire doubled in size to take in India and Australia, among other nations. She also became the first modern monarch, in that the power of the House of Commons increased under her reign at the expense of the royal family. In 1840, she married her cousin Prince Albert and although the British public never really took Albert to their hearts, she clearly did: she had nine kids with him!

In 1861, he died of typhoid and Victoria went into such deep mourning she became a virtual recluse and became known as the "widow of Windsor" before retiring to the Isle of Wight. *EastEnders*' scriptwriters couldn't have dreamt up a more depressing ending.

# Stephenson's Rocket!

Treat for trainspotters as trains are invented

What did trainspotters do with their time before the invention of the modern locomotive? Hmm, the mind boggles... Anyway, in 1829 George Stephenson put them out of their misery when his revolutionary "Rocket" train signalled the beginning of rail travel as we know it. Liverpool and Manchester Railways had launched the Rainhill Trials – to find the fastest locomotive in Britain – and the Rocket won.

A year later at the official opening of the railway, William Huskisson MP was killed when the Rocket ran over his left leg. Thus the fledgling British Rail was granted its first excuse: "Ladies and gentlemen, your 8:54 from Liverpool to Manchester has been delayed due to an MP's limb on the line."

# Breaking the chains

Slavery is abolished

If at first you don't succeed, try, try again. Luckily, William Wilberforce lived by this maxim and he introduced anti-slavery motions in Parliament for 18 years running before his campaign bore fruit. Influenced by anti-slavery campaigner Thomas Clarkson, Wilberforce and his supporters plugged and plugged away until 1807, when Parliament abolished slavery in Britain. Then, in 1833, slavery was also abolished across the whole British Empire. Sadly, Wilberforce had died a month earlier but the legacy of his work would last forever.

Wilberforce had also worked tirelessly for the Association for the Better Observance of Sunday, which aimed to provide religious reading material for youngsters. Blimey, if he didn't make it to heaven, who the hell will?

# Rule Britannia!

Brits take over the whole world (well, nearly)

You know how it is: sometimes, you get on a bit of a roll and suddenly everything but everything is going your way? Well, that's exactly what happened to Britain in the 1800s as the world finally acknowledged a fundamental truth: we rock!

People around the world got hooked on the novels of the great Charles Dickens and if his success created great expectations then other Brits were not to let the side down. In the same period, Isambard Kingdom Brunel – who had already created the Great Western Railway and built the Clifton Suspension Bridge – designed the first transatlantic steam ship, another great British present to the world. No surprise, then, that the Great Exhibition – held in 1851 in a glass palace in Hyde Park – was dominated by British innovations.

Meanwhile, the British Empire expanded throughout the century. New territory was secured across the globe including in India and South America. It was as if the Brits were saying, "Have you had enough, world, or do you want some more? Eh? Do you? DO YOU?!" And they did.

# Lady with the Lamp

Florence Nightingale heals the world

Tut! Women, eh? Can't organise anything… Stop, right there! That's exactly the sort of chauvinistic attitude that Florence Nightingale thoroughly disproved during her pioneering career as a nurse.

Nightingale's finest hour was when she was sent to the Crimean War in October 1854. Arriving on horseback in Turkey, she treated more than 2,000 patients and slashed mortality rates by improving hygiene and reorganising patient care. Her arrival was greeted with annoyance by some male doctors but everyone had to stand back in awe as she rolled up her sleeves and masterminded the whole operation.

Although the famous image of her as the Lady with the Lamp, mopping the brows of wounded soldiers persists, she was actually a hard-headed, administrative expert and also arranged the finances of soldiers, wrote letters to their families for them and reorganised the military hospitals. They could do with a few of her sort over at Holby City these days.

# Salt and vinegar with that?

The fish 'n' chips trade starts

The olden days must have really sucked. As old photographs prove, the world was black and white and all men had curly moustaches. But the world became a lot less rubbish in the 1800s when (drum roll) the first fish and chip shop opened in England!

Step forward and take a bow, Mr Joseph Malin who opened the first chippy in London in 1860. Fried fish and fried potatoes had actually been sold separately in England for some time before this. Charles Dickens mentioned a fried fish warehouse in 1838's *Oliver Twist*, while up north, fried potato chips had already been on sale for a while.

Since Malin opened his establishment in London, visits to the chippy have become both a tradition and a treat for Brits. Seafronts around the country are dotted with fish and chip shops and town centres resound with folk being asked if they want their cod and chips "open or wrapped". The Harry Ramsden chain alone serves more than 20,000 portions every day. Visitors to these shores enjoy sampling fish and chips – even controversial US president George W. Bush tucked into a portion when he visited Sedgefield in 2003. Pickled onion or a gherkin, sir?

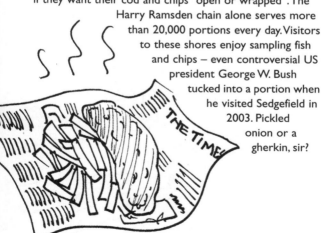

# Sporting firsts

Brits discover the joy of competitive sport

Had the hype-tastic Sky Sports existed in the olden days, it would have found the 19th century to be ridiculously exciting because Britain went sport-mad during this period. Although all four sports already existed in different forms, it was the 1800s that saw the birth proper of football, cricket, rugby and greyhound racing.

Until 1876, greyhounds raced only as part of a hunt, but that year saw them race on a track for the first time in Hendon. Meanwhile, in public schools across Britain, posh boys were playing the games that came to develop into football and rugby. While the toffs stuck with rugby, they soon gave football to the working classes (only returning in the 1990s when *Fever Pitch* author Nick Hornby explained it was okay to do so). Meanwhile, a proper cricket County Championship was formed.

And so it was that Britain gave these fine sports to the world – and sat back while the rest of the world worked out how to beat us at them.

"Bet you this will catch on... "

# It's not all right, Jack

Ripper goes on slaying spree

**CHARLES DICKENS:
MY ATKINS DIET HELL**

Monday 18th August, 1888     Ha'penny

## EXCLUSIVE
By our crime correspondent

# JACK THE LAD STRIKES AGAIN!

Be very afraid! An artist's impression
of the shadowy fiend on the loose.

Cops were baffled last night as a FIFTH prostitute was slayed in the Whitechapel area of East London. Unable to apprehend the callous killing crim – dubbed Jack the Ripper – detectives are investigating theories that the killer could be a doctor – or even linked to the Royal Family! SEE PAGES 2, 3, 4, 5, 6, 7, 8 AND SPECIAL PULL-OUT IN CENTRE-PAGES.

*INSIDE:* **QUEEN VIC: I USED TO BE A GEEZER!
ROBBIE WILLIAMS: I'M DEPRESSED AGAIN!**

# Spreading the love... or hate

Marmite is invented

Author Bill Bryson says you have to be British to appreciate Marmite and he is probably right. Although the savoury spread is sold in other parts of the world, its main purchasers are ex-pats. Yet again, Brits are showing that we are the arbiters not just of good taste but also, frankly, moral superiority.

Marmite was launched in Burton-upon-Trent, Staffordshire in 1902 and within five years a second factory was built to meet demand. Its makers never looked back and it is now a national institution, while ex-pats around the globe have jars of it sent to them to remind them of home.

The advertisements for the yeast extract spread have been most imaginative down the years including "The growing up spread you never grow out of", "My mate, Marmite" and more recently the "I love/I hate Marmite" campaigns. While it is true that this tangy, almost inedible spread is loved by some and hated by others, we're here to say that those who hate it are just plain wrong.

# Ice with that?

Titanic toppled

"It's practically unsinkable," boasted the builders of the *Titanic*, which turned out to be a bit like saying "Jack the Ripper? Just a misunderstood soul!" or "Nuclear bombs? Pah, wouldn't hurt a fly."

Built at the Harland & Wolff shipyard in Belfast, the Titanic was the largest passenger ship in the world at the time and had all manner of posh features including a Turkish bath, library and squash court. Great facilities, but as it set out from Southampton for its maiden voyage on April 10, 1912, it turned out that its passengers were going to become rather more interested in its canvas lifeboats. It hit an iceberg and sank within a few hours. Only 706 of the 2,223 people aboard survived, which meant 1,517 perished.

Since then, the *Titanic* has become a by-word for failure and "to rearrange the deckchairs on the *Titanic*" is to undertake an entirely futile task, as in: to expect to be able to endure the dreadful, overlong Hollywood film *Titanic* without sobbing with boredom is a bit like trying to rearrange the deckchairs on the *Titanic*.

# Girl Power Pt 1

The suffragettes win the vote

Hell hath no fury like a woman scorned but the suffragettes proved that there are few furies as, erm, furious as those of women who are discriminated against.

Starting in 1897, the National Union of Woman's Suffrage worked mainly peacefully to try and get women the vote. In the early 1900s, the gloves came off as angry suffragettes smashed windows in Oxford Street, chained themselves to Buckingham Palace, vandalised golf courses and firebombed churches and politicians' homes for good measure.

Then in 1913, Emily Davison threw herself under King George V's horse at the Derby race. Imprisoned suffragettes went on hunger strike, but the government instructed prison bosses to force-feed them to make sure no one died and became a martyr figure.

The breakthrough came after World War 1 ended, as women's roles in the war were recognised. In 1918, women over the age of 30 who owned property were granted the vote and 10 years later, all women over the age of 21 were given the vote too. Yay!

# War, huh? What is it good for?

The bloody misery of World War I

As the 5.5 million-strong British army was waved off at the outset of World War I, many believed the fighting would be over in months. Four years later, the fighting finally ended and the casualties were counted.

The British fought the Germans and Turks on land and at sea but the most enduring image of the war will always be the battles in the trenches which took place across Europe starting from 1914. Poison gas was introduced by the Germans and the British and French soon returned the compliment. Neither side was able to score a decisive victory in the first round of battles but many men were lost.

The plan for the Battle of the Somme in 1918 was to flatten the German trenches with a sustained attack. Although 1.6 million shells were fired, the German

trenches were deep and sturdy enough to sustain most of their men. With the shelling over, the Germans emerged from their trenches and opened fire on the startled British troops. By the end of the first day alone, the British suffered 60,000 casualties, of whom one-third died, and the battle ultimately saw 420,000 Brits injured or killed. Many were volunteers taking part in their first big battle. Some of the young men who survived described the battle as hell on earth.

After further fighting, on November 11, 1918, the Allies and the Germans finally agreed to a ceasefire and the war ended. More than three million young British men were either killed, wounded or lost during the war. And that's why this is a story without a funny punchline.

# Auntie pops round

The British Broadcasting Corporation is founded

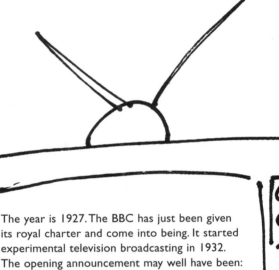

The year is 1927. The BBC has just been given its royal charter and come into being. It started experimental television broadcasting in 1932. The opening announcement may well have been: "Welcome to the BBC. Coming up later, tiresome Spanish shenanigans in *Eldorado*, Esther Rantzen goofily laughs at some vegetables that look like genitals in *That's Life*, cockneys sit around moaning on *EastEnders*, Jonathan Ross interviews Sharon Osbourne's daughter again and Moira Stewart gets a new hairstyle every time she reads the news. But first, *One Foot In The Grave*... "

# Yanks for the memories

King Edward VIII abdicates to wed his American belle

You are the monarch of England and you're in love with an American divorcee, but the Church of England and political establishment won't let you marry her. Face it, we've all been there. But Edward VIII was there first!

Newspaper headlines around the world screamed with horror at the King's love affair with Wallis Simpson – well, they weren't to know that what Fergie, Charles and the rest would dish up in the 1980s would make this episode seem like small potatoes.

Anyway, Edward followed his heart and abdicated so he could marry the love of his life. His younger brother George VI took the throne and Edward and Wallis married in France on June 3, 1937 and lived in Paris. Aw, sweet.

# We'll fight them on the beaches!

Winston proves that the Hun don't like it up 'em

Neville Chamberlain must have felt pretty chuffed when he emerged from the Munich Conference in 1938 having secured peace with Hitler – until Hitler invaded Poland a few months later and World War II was underway.

The early battles took place in the Norwegian waters where English-laid mines destroyed lots of Hitler's ships. After the British were forced to evacuate Dunkirk, Chamberlain left office and was replaced by Winston Churchill. He promised "blood, toil, tears and sweat" and vowed never to surrender. Fighting talk, and his actions lived up to it.

Then came the Battle of Britain when cities across Britain from Exeter to Glasgow and Belfast took heavy punishment from German bombers. However, the RAF destroyed the German air force in September 1940. When the Americans joined forces with the British, they were able to flatten German cities with Dresden taking an especially thorough battering in a firestorm.

"We'll fight them on the beaches," Churchill had promised, and this came true on June 6, 1944 – D-Day – when more than three million troops crossed the English Channel to Normandy and together with their Allies ultimately brought Hitler to his knees. On VE Day, May 3, 1945, millions celebrated in Britain, most notably in Trafalgar Square and on the Mall. Together with the reigning monarchs, Winston Churchill appeared on the balcony of Buckingham Palace and the whole country shouted: "Good work, fella!"

# The queue starts here

The NHS is founded

Before 1948, if you were ill in Britain then you had to hope you were either rich or lived near some of the hospitals that were run by charities. Otherwise, you were in trouble. Then, Labour minister Aneurin "Nye" Bevan brought in the National Health Service and health care became free for everyone! Hurrah!

Bevan faced bitter opposition from doctors, who thought the NHS would destroy their incomes, and from the Conservative Party, who were just being, erm, the Conservative Party. Once the NHS came into being, it proved so popular that it had to keep expanding and expanding to deal with the demand – a problem that no one has quite got on top of to this day.

Final word goes to Bevan, who described the Tories who opposed the founding of the NHS as "lower than vermin". Steady on, old boy!

# Orwell's vision

Big Brother is watching you

Astrologers Mystic Meg and Russell Grant have trousered a few bob by predicting the future but even these heavyweight literary giants would have to bow to the example of George Orwell, who in 1949 published the allegorical political novel *Nineteen Eighty-Four*. The book outlined a nightmarish view of Britain's future where "Big Brother" is watching you and where a brutal state enforces obedience among a public terrified of the notorious Room 101.

Did Orwell call it right? Well, a couple of decades on from that date, we are probably watching *Big Brother* more than it is watching us and *Room 101* is merely a show for ailing celebs to sit obediently as the host makes wisecracks; it's pretty poor but nothing to be genuinely terrified of.

However, through this novel and his previous work *Animal Farm*, Orwell – real name Eric Arthur Blair – secured himself a regular place in political discussion, where references to "Big Brother", "Orwellian society" and "everyone being equal but some being more equal than others" are commonplace. And – grossly unjust as it seems – not even Russell Grant can boast that.

# Lizzie gets the top job

The coronation of Queen Elizabeth II

Say you became the monarch of England – you'd expect some pretty impressive presents, wouldn't you? So imagine Queen Elizabeth II's disappointment when, during her coronation, she was handed an orb, a sceptre, the rod of mercy and a royal ring of sapphires and rubies. No iPods, no Playstations… rubbish, eh? But those were the four symbols of authority she was handed in front of more than 8,000 guests at Westminster Abbey on June 2, 1953.

An estimated 20 million people watched the BBC's coverage of the day and a further three million lined the streets of London to catch a glimpse of the new monarch. The Queen replaced her father, King George VI, who had died 16 months earlier. The formal coronation was delayed so there could be nice weather for the occasion and people up and down the country took advantage to have a nice day off work, throw street parties and generally let their hair down. Hurrah!

# Canal surgery

The Suez Crisis

A British government flying in the face of mass public
opposition to attack an aggressor in the Middle East –
hmm, sounds familiar, doesn't it? But the difference
between the Suez Crisis and the Iraq War was that in the
former, France went to battle alongside Britain and it was
the USA who opposed military action (George W. Bush
was only 10 years old at this point).

In 1956, Egypt's General Nasser decided to nationalise
the Suez Canal, which had been previously run by the
British and the French. In October, the British and French
were joined by Israel in attacking Egypt (are you
following?). Already facing opposition at home and from
the USA, Prime Minister Anthony Eden was then warned
by the Russians that they would nuke London if the
attackers didn't desist. He decided to
pull out – well, you would,
wouldn't you?

This episode provided
the final confirmation that
global power had shifted
from England to the
Americans and Russians.
Mr Eden resigned
shortly after
in shame. Ah, those
were the days. When
politicians actually
felt shame.

# Currying favour

Chicken tikka masala is invented. Whoo-hoo!

Marks & Spencer sell 18 tonnes of it per week and 1.19 billion portions of it are sold in Indian restaurants every year. Little wonder then that politician Robin Cook claimed that chicken tikka masala is our national dish.

The origins of the dish are somewhat contentious, but the earliest mention of it is in Glasgow in the 1950s, when a diner at a restaurant asked: "Where's my gravy?" when served a plate of chicken tikka. The inventive chef added some creamy tomato soup and some spices and a new dish was born.

Robin Cook wasn't just referring to the dish's popularity, he was also underlining how Britain absorbs and adapts external influences. Indian restaurant waiters might somewhat disagree with Cook's view of the harmonious influence of curry when the pubs empty through their doors on a Friday night, but there is no doubt that chicken tikka masala is a legendary, and very British, if actually Indian dish. Is that clear?

# Spies like us

The Cambridge ring

It is safe to say that paranoia and suspicion reigned among intelligence agencies during the Cold War. Or is it? Were they just pretending to be paranoid and suspicious to throw us off the scent?

A group of Cambridge University students were approached by the KGB in the 1930s and agreed to work for the Soviet Union. All of them rose to influential positions in the British government and intelligence services. The Soviets couldn't have asked for more helpful spies. Or could they? Was it not possible that, rather than deceiving the British to help the Soviets, these men were doing a double-bluff and rather than giving British secrets to the Soviets, were giving Soviet secrets to the British? Confused? So are we.

In truth, these boffins were hugely helpful spies for the KGB and they leaked many of the British government's secrets. In 1951, two of them – Guy Burgess and Donald Maclean – publicly defected to the Soviet Union.

# Sex! Politics! Dog bowls!

The Profumo affair

You want political corruption? Politicians at sex parties with men in masks eating out of a dog bowl? Fancy throwing some Russian attachés and FBI investigations into the mix? And how about the downfall of a British Prime Minister? Then you've turned to the right page.

The Profumo affair was one of the biggest political scandals ever and was sparked when Cabinet minister John Profumo had a brief fling with showgirl Christine Keeler. Married politician has affair… hmm, hardly unheard of, is it? What made the Profumo affair so scandalous was that Keeler was also having a fling with a Soviet spy. With such a potential threat to British security, questions were asked of Profumo and he made the mistake of lying to the House of Commons. He eventually came clean and resigned. Then the FBI started their own investigation. Soon after, the Prime Minister Harold Macmillan had to go walkies out of the door too after the whole affair made him ill. Woof, woof!

# Mods v. rockers

Oh, we do like to scrap beside the seaside...

The English seaside over the Whitsun weekend in late spring. The beautiful, warming sunshine, the rhythmical sound of the waves rolling gently into the bay... I say: what's that on the horizon? Why, it's a bloody great scrap between thousands of members of rival youth cults!

In the mid-'60s, mods (designer suits, mopeds) and rockers (leather jackets, huge quiffs, motorbikes) fought running battles on British beaches, scenes that were later immortalised in the film *Quadrophenia*. The ageing residents of Bournemouth, Margate, Hastings and Brighton all witnessed nasty old scraps as profanities and deckchairs filled the air and the police waded in. A lot of sharp suits were slashed and big quiffs dented along the way.

# Ban the bomb

The anti-nuclear movement is born

Nuclear weapons don't really appeal to the British sense of fair play, do they? Whole cities get wiped out in a split second and every single person standing in the way gets instantly vaporised. And then there's the dreadful bore of the nuclear winter that follows a month or so later. It's just not cricket, is it?

So as Britain scrambled to join the arms race in the 1950s, the Campaign for Nuclear Disarmament (CND) was launched with a huge public meeting in London followed by a march to a nuclear research facility in Aldermaston. Before long the CND badge was the most recognisable political campaign logo in the world and CND the biggest protest movement. Naturally, during the 1960s the group got, like, particularly big because, like, the long-haired, sandal-wearing hippies of the hour thought nuclear weapons were, like, really heavy, man? Which, to be fair, is an understatement.

# Crossing the line

Excellent decision helps England win World Cup

Sometimes in life, it is important, nay vital, to look at the bigger picture and not get bogged down in the small details. So let us look at that bigger picture. As hosts for the 1966 World Cup, England swept to the final in style. Indeed, Alf Ramsey's team didn't even concede a goal until the semi-final against Portugal. And so to the final against West Germany at Wembley Stadium. Some 93,000 spectators – including the Queen and Prince Philip – packed Wembley to watch England win 4–2 and land the World Cup for the first time. As stated, we must look at the bigger picture as England fans always have when controversial decisions have robbed their team of progress. For instance, when Diego Maradona's "Hand of God" scored against England in the 1986 World Cup Finals we didn't complain for a moment and it's never even been mentioned since (honest).

So quite why certain people make so much about whether or not Sir Geoffrey Hurst of West Ham's second goal against West Germany went over the line is beyond us.

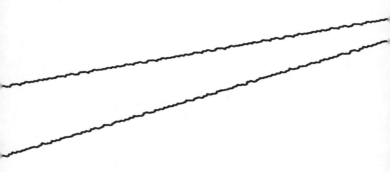

# Beatlemania

The Fab Four and the Swinging Sixties!

Okay, turn off your mind, relax and float downstream and back to the Sixties, man, when four lads from Liverpool called John, Paul, George and Ringo were totally ruling the world.

Everywhere The Beatles went, there were, like, huge crowds of girls screaming and falling at their feet. Their worldwide fanbase was unprecedented. To this day, rock bands around the world concede their debt to The Beatles.

Britain was really rocking out, and each year, thousands would put flowers in their hair and turn up for the Isle of Wight festival where the likes of Bob Dylan and Jimi Hendrix would perform. Free love, cool tunes and loads to smoke: no wonder so many thousands flocked to the festival and others like it.

And wow, man, look up at the sky! Lucy is up there with some diamonds! Turn on, tune in and drop out: the 1960s were farrrrr out, man.

# Spit, snot and Sid!

Punk rock and the Jubilee!

Burn those flares and glittery tops, stick a pin through your nose, rip up your clothes, dye your hair green and jump up and down a lot – it's time for punk rock! In 1977, angry bands, fast, loud and often tuneless songs booted the glam rockers, hippies and prog-rockers out of the public eye and a new youth cult was born.

Punk tore up the rule books of music and stamped all over the remains of it. If you spat at a band, that was a mark of respect, guitars were there to be thrashed at not tuned, and the uglier and noisier you were, the better!

The best-known punk act was the Sex Pistols. One day in 1977 the band caused uproar when they swore on a tea-time television programme – and having offended so many, they never looked back! They released an anti-monarchy song, ironically entitled *God Save the Queen*, to mark Elizabeth II's Silver Jubilee and promptly got banned by radio and television.

In keeping with its live-fast-die-young ethos, punk rock was over very quickly but a few old punks wouldn't give up the ghost and for many years hung around on Chelsea's Kings Road. Their spiky Mohicans and studded leather jackets made them a popular photo-opportunity for visiting tourists. You big sell-outs!

# Trouble and strife

The Royal weddings… and the aftermath

On July 29, 1981, 3,500 invited guests and one billion television viewers saw Lady Diana Spencer become the first English woman to marry the heir to the throne since 1659 when she wed Prince Charles. We watched her walk up the aisle at Westminster Abbey. The couple swapped vows and she blushed. Later, they appeared on the balcony of Buckingham Palace and kissed to cheers across the nation.

Five years on, another royal wedding took place at the Abbey when Prince Andrew married Sarah Ferguson. With both couples married, everything was in place for years of infidelity, sucked toes, bulimia, bugged telephone calls, and a divorce. Aw, what a lovely fairytale – an example to us all.

# Cereal thrillers

Brits get square eyes as breakfast telly is launched

It is shocking to recall – and any kids reading should brace themselves – but once upon a time, there was no television in the mornings. Instead of slouching in front of the box, human beings used instead to find other ways to pass the mornings, like talking to one another, preparing and enjoying extravagant breakfasts and even occasionally managing to leave on time for work or school. [Seems unlikely. Can you check this? Ed.]

Well all of that stuff got booted firmly into touch in 1983 when the BBC launched *Breakfast Time* and ITV launched *Good Morning Britain*. Suddenly, our small screens were full of the likes of Sir David Frost and Frank Bough wearing brightly-knitted sweaters, the Green Goddess and Mad Lizzie doing two-minute workouts and Roland Rat saying: "Nnnyyeaaaaaaaaaahhhh!" a lot.

Before long, the magazine format of these shows was rolled out over much of the day as daytime television became a daily ritual for mums, grannies and lazy students. Shows like *This Morning with Richard & Judy* and *Trisha* owe their existence to the breakfast television model. Frank Bough's jumper has a lot to answer for.

# The Iron Lady

Maggie Thatcher becomes Britain's first female PM

"No! No! No!" – mere mortals like us only get to say that when we are asked whether we want fries, ketchup and to supersize at McDonald's. Margaret Thatcher got to say it while giving European politicians a good handbagging! That'll be because she was Britain's first female Prime Minister.

A grocer's daughter from Lincolnshire, Maggie came to power on May 4, 1979 and the British public said "Yes! Yes! Yes!" to her as she won three general elections for the Conservative Party. Her term of office was defined by deregulation, reduced public spending, lower taxation, and privatisation. The Falklands War, miners' strike and the poll tax caused most controversy and when she left office in 1990, half the nation wept with her and half had a good old giggle.

We all have reason to thank Maggie, though, because as a research chemist in her younger days, she was a member of the team that developed soft frozen ice cream for the first time. Cool.

# And they call it yuppie love

Thatcher's children come of age and clean up

If you took a walk in any city centre during the 1980s, chances are you got barged out of the way by a cocksure young man with a filofax in one hand and a breeze-block-sized mobile phone in the other.

Yuppies, their name taken from "Young Urban Professional", were young men – rarely women – who rampaged their way through the decade making a tidy fortune along the way. They spent so much time flaunting themselves around cocktail bars, playing testosterone-fuelled games of squash and whizzing around in their BMWs that you might have wondered how they found the time to make so much cash. The answer is that they made their fortune through non-time-consuming careers like share-trading and banking (and most of them really were right w…, er, bankers). The epitome of 1980s Britain, nothing was going to get in their way. Speaking of which, tell Bertie I'm on my way… TAXI!

# Feed the world

Live Aid raises millions

Filling Wembley Stadium with 72,000 people and encouraging them to sing along to a song about Christmas in the middle of July seems, on the face of it, to be a ridiculous idea. But Live Aid, a mahoosive charity concert in 1985, was actually a stroke of genius.

Organised by Bob Geldof and Midge Ure to raise funds for famine relief in Ethiopia, it netted £150 million and united the entire nation in one common purpose and was the inspiration for the Live8 concerts 20 years on.

Not that it was just a British event: on the same day, 90,000 people attended the other Live Aid concert in the JFK Stadium in Philadelphia and 1.5 billion television viewers watched the concerts in 100 countries across the globe. Highlights on the day included Queen's magnificent set, Phil Collins's egotistical transatlantic flight so he could perform at both stadiums – it's all about me! – and too many dodgy haircuts and technical hitches to even begin to list here.

Most memorable, though, was Geldof losing his patience during a mid-afternoon TV interview, swearing and thumping his fist on the table as he implored viewers to donate more money. You tell 'em, Bob!

# Wrong kind of leaves

Rail madness reaches new levels

Never mind Live Aid and Africa, passengers on British trains in the 1980s could have been forgiven for thinking that they were living in a Third World country themselves. As trains across the country either arrived late or were cancelled altogether, a series of bizarre excuses were rolled out by rail bosses. In the winter, passengers were told "the wrong kind of snow" was holding up their trains, then in the autumn, "leaves on the track" managed to bring most of Britain's rail services to a standstill. Still, at least the summer didn't create any excuses, eh? Not so fast – the sun was occasionally "too warm for the tracks". So railway bosses only had to worry about a short spell in mid-spring where they would run out of excuses. Otherwise, they had it pretty much covered.

# Firms and headhunters

Football hooliganism really kicks off

"Come and 'ave a go if you fink you're 'ard enuf!"
Actually, old boys, if it's all the same to you please don't
come and 'ave a go because we're pretty darn sure we're
not 'ard enuf. Nowadays, football fans are a relatively
polite bunch and most scandals in the sport tend to
involve the players, so it may come as something of a
shock for you to learn that once upon a time, the
players on the field were paragons of moral substance
compared to some of the loons who watched them
from the terraces.

Throughout the late 1970s and 1980s, football
hooliganism was an ugly scar on the beautiful game.
Fights between rival gangs regularly "went off" in our
stadiums and when the England team travelled abroad,
hooligans often followed and spectacularly
redecorated the cities they were visiting. This
made following football a rather dangerous
hobby for the peaceful folk who made up
the majority of football fans. It took
tragedies at the Heysel Stadium in
Brussels and Hillsborough
Stadium in Sheffield for the
authorities to finally address
hooliganism and the problem is
now vaguely under control in
Britain. Which is nice.

# Tell Sid!

Maggie privatises everything

If the 1970s was the decade of strikes, the winter of discontent and Trade Union power, the 1980s was the decade when the balance tipped the other way. In her second term of office, Maggie Thatcher privatised British Telecom and British Gas and then pretty much everything else she could get her hands on. Or, rather, get her hands off.

Before long, one in four Brits owned shares and 40 former state-owned businesses had been privatised. These included British Gas, and when that was flogged off, we even got a television advertisement series in which people told each other that if they saw Sid, they must tell him that he could buy shares in British Gas.

Privatisation changed the economics of Britain profoundly and even influenced our television ad breaks. A year later, a commercial soap opera of a different kind kicked off with the Gold Blend coffee couple flirting for what felt like decades. Just get a room, you two!

# Failure rules!

Eddie the Eagle soars... and lands not very far away

Had Michael Edwards done reasonably well at the 1998 Winter Olympics, nobody would remember his name. Actually, even if he'd won a gold medal, he would not be remembered as fondly as he is now. We Brits love a loser and there were few greater British losers than the man who became known as "Eddie the Eagle" Edwards.

A bespectacled plasterer from Cheltenham, Edwards qualified for the 1988 ski-jump category merely because no other Briton applied. He arrived at the Olympics late after his plane was delayed and his suitcase split open on the airport carousel, sending his belongings everywhere. On the piste, he was much fatter than any of his competitors and his glasses kept steaming up which meant he was effectively blind for much of the competition. Like a blindfolded, drunken elephant, he made a total mess of his attempts to ski-jump and finished a resounding last in his category.

However, Edwards captured the hearts of a nation and became a hero for his spectacular failure. Since the Olympics he has declared himself bankrupt, done some building in Gloucester and studied law. A Hollywood movie, *Eddie the Eagle*, was released in 2016. Go, Eddie!

# The PM is knifed

Maggie, Maggie, Maggie! Out, out out!

A quick quiz question for you: you have led your party through a period of spectacular success and won three general elections on the trot – what happens next? You get stabbed in the back, of course! This is politics we are talking about!

In 1990, after a series of rows with Maggie Thatcher over the European Union, Michael Heseltine MP threw down the gauntlet and challenged her for the leadership. She failed to secure enough votes to see him off and eventually backed out, allowing her preferred successor, a very dull man whose name escapes us, to become PM.

She wept on the doorstep of Number 10 on her final day but as she left she warned: "I shall be a very good back-seat driver." For years after, her appearances at Conservative Party conferences would overshadow her immediate successor, who was called, um... can't remember... and indeed subsequent party leaders whose names were... oh, who cares?

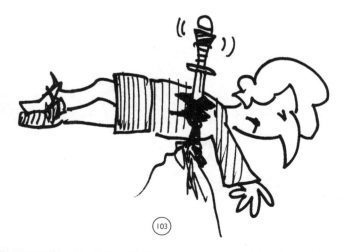

# Cool Britannia!

Things could only get better… apparently

Whatever your political leanings, you can't deny that the evening of the 1997 general election was full of drama. David Mellor and Michael Portillo lost their seats, Labour won a landslide victory and then ministers including John Prescott and Peter Mandelson had a little jig at the Royal Festival Hall party.

"Cool" is not a word you'd easily associate with their dancing efforts but it did sum up the mood of Britain in the mid-1990s. Oasis and Blur were at the peak of their Britpop powers, a new wave of young artists was filling our galleries with their work and even the England football team was playing some sexy stuff.

New PM Tony Blair was cunning enough to exploit this sense of well-being and invited a party full of celebrities to Downing Street for a post-election celebration. He also got photographed playing his electric guitar. Which was about as embarrassing as watching an uncle trying to dance at his teenage niece's birthday party.

# Three lions on a shirt

England come close at Euro 96

In the days leading up to the 1996 European Championship, which was staged in England, the host football team came under fire from the press. Terry Venables's players were attacked for some boozy nights out that included Paul Gascoigne and Co. being photographed downing cocktails in the "dentist's" chair in a Hong Kong nightclub.

Fortunately, the lads shrugged off the criticism and put on the best performance by an England team since 1966. Highlights included the 2–0 defeat of Scotland (where Gazza scored a brilliant goal and tactfully reprised the dentist's chair incident to celebrate) and the 4–1 demolition of Holland that saw the English play the Dutch masters off the park.

And so to the semi-final: as the rules of international football dictate, England went out after a penalty shoot-out. However, during the "golden goal" extra-time period earlier in that tie, Gazza just failed to convert a certain goal when his penalty-box lunge missed the ball by a few inches. By, indeed, the width of a kebab, one of his favourite foods. So remember, kids – if you want to make it in football, say no to doners.

# Girl Power Pt 2

The Spice Girls go pop

The suffragettes won women the vote and Germaine Greer inspired ladies across the globe with her feminist writings, but the real historical phenomenon that empowered the fairer sex was, of course, the Spice Girls and their innovative concept of "Girl Power". Ginger, Sporty, Posh, Scary and Baby really taught male chauvinist pigs a thing or two by wearing short skirts, platform heels and singing: "I wanna, I wanna, I wanna, I wanna, I wanna, I really really really really wanna zig-a-zig-ah."

The band formed in 1994 and became the biggest-selling girl group of all time, shifting 45 million albums and 30 million singles. Also, with their, ahem, attainable looks and, well, somewhat modest singing abilities they gave hope to every daydreaming supermarket checkout girl across Britain that they, too, could become pop stars. So it is no coincidence that it was the Spice Girls' manager, Simon Fuller, who launched the first *Pop Idol* television series the year after the girls split. Great.

# Candle in the wind

"Queen of hearts" Diana dies

Few events in history have united Britain so much as the death of Diana, Princess of Wales, in 1997. The nation was plunged into unprecedented mourning as news emerged that the Princess had died alongside Dodi Al Fayed in a car crash in Paris in the early hours of the morning.

A week of mourning followed, but within the nation's grief was a degree of anger. Questions were asked of the paparazzi who had pursued Diana for years and the nation demanded that the Queen and the rest of the Royal Family show more respect to Diana's memory. However, Tony Blair and Sir Elton John managed to capture the public mood, Blair by dubbing Diana "the people's princess" and Sir Elton by singing *Candle in the Wind* at her funeral and twitching his eyebrow a lot.

The public display of grief marked a dramatic softening of the British upper lip and the tragedy forced the Royal Family to undergo a subtle but definite modernisation process.

# What a spectacle!

Harry Potter arrives

Nowadays, when we are enduring the boredom of a long train journey, we pass the time by picking up our mobile phones, ringing everyone we've ever met and yelling at them: "Yeah, I'm on the train." But in 1991, on a train from Manchester to London, J. K. Rowling was suddenly struck with inspiration. "Here," she thought, "why don't I write a book about a boy called Harry Potter?"

Why not, indeed? Around 450 million book sales worldwide and several lucrative film adaptations later, Rowling is now reckoned to be richer than the Queen. Who would have thought that a story about a boy with glasses would grip people's imagination across the globe and become a top brand? It's hard now to imagine life without Harry and his friends, without the midnight parties at bookshops as each instalment is launched, without the films playing to packed cinemas. At least the Potter series has encouraged kids (and adults) away from their Playstations and back into bookshops again. Hurrah!

# Shock and war

Brit PM supports US president

We've all developed a bit of a crush in our time. You know how it is, you can't concentrate on anything, don't really want to eat and you find it hard to sleep properly. It can mess with your head, so perhaps it was Tony Blair's love affair with George W. Bush that affected his judgement over the controversial Iraq War?

Perhaps it was Bush's, ahem, amazing intellect that first turned Blair's head. After all, Bush has in his time opined that "We cannot let our terrorists hold this nation hostile or hold our allies hostile"; and that "America's enemies are innovative and resourceful, and so are we. They never stop thinking about new ways to harm our country and our people, and neither do we."

Bush and Blair's relationship has brought Britain and the USA closer than ever, which has caused some concern, but at least they both believe in something because, as Bush rightly stated, "If you don't stand for anything, you don't stand for anything!" You tell 'em, Dubya.

# Panic on the streets!

Everyone gangs up on hoodies and chavs

Back in the olden days, Robin Hood is supposed to have robbed the rich to feed the poor. In modern times, "hoodies" are supposed to be robbing the rich, the poor and everyone else in between. In modern Britain, when the press are not scaring us all about terrorists and asylum seekers, they terrify us that teenagers wearing hooded jumpers and baseball caps are going to rob us all of everything we've ever owned.

A new 21st-century crime of "happy-slapping" has become associated with hoodies, whereby people are beaten up and their battering is filmed on mobile phones and texted around. Kind of like *You've Been Framed* but with a sinister edge. As panic spread, the Bluewater Shopping Centre in Kent banned people wearing baseball caps and hooded jumpers – which immediately made monk customers worry that their hoods would put them on the banned list.

Also accused of anti-social behaviour are "chavs", which is the label the media have applied to working-class people who wear counterfeit Burberry and bling jewellery. Much of this only really amounts to a new form of snobbery. A nation of chavs would no doubt respond: "Am I bovvered?"

# Interest sinks to a record low

Financial crash leads to tighter economic era

Mortgage holders love 'em, savers hate 'em – since 2009, Britain has lived in an era of record low interest rates.

Following the financial crash of 2008, the Bank of England cut its bank rate from 5% to a historic low of just 0.5%. The move came as Britain faced a lengthy economic depression, after Northern Rock was nationalised, and other banks, including RBS and Lloyds, were rescued by mega taxpayer bailouts.

Savers begged policy-setters to raise rates again, but for years their pleas fell on deaf ears, as the rates stayed stubbornly at their historic low. Although there were occasional rumours they may go up again, these hopes were dashed as simultaneous whispers were aired that they might be lowered further, to negative interest rates.

Post-crash Britain has sparked a new set of clichés in Britain. Talk of "tightening our belts", "living within our means", and the supposed "trickle down" of wealth echoed around the place, as the great British public nearly had kittens over financial security.

# The duck island and moat-cleaning

MPs expenses claims are exposed

What do a duck island, horse manure and a toilet seat have in common? No, they are not items on a Heston Blumenthal tasting menu. They were just three of the bizarre items that MPs claimed expenses for in 21st century Britain.

In 2009, the lid was blown off widespread abuse of the allowances and expenses system. As taxpayer anger grew, there were sackings, resignations and repayments. Some MPs and peers were even jailed.

The aforementioned instances were Sir Peter Viggers' attempt to claim £1,645 for a duck island at his Hampshire home, Derek Conway's bid to get the taxpayer to pay £97 for two toilet seats, and David Heathcoat-Amory's £380 horse manure claim.

Then there was Douglas Hogg, the Tory MP who claimed £2,200 expenses to clean the moat on his country estate – a richly symbolic moment.

The revelation that so many elected representatives were milking the system caused an unprecedented storm to break over Westminster. Prime minister Gordon Brown eventually tried to apologise to the country "on behalf of all politicians", but by then much of the British public was beyond being placated.

# Ukip if you want to...

The fall and rise of Nigel Farage

During the 2010 election campaign, Nigel Farage flew a light aircraft over Buckingham, with a Ukip banner trailing behind the plane. The stunt went a tad wrong when the plane nosedived and crashed into a field. Farage emerged from the wreckage, bloodied but unbowed. It had been just another eventful day at the office for the populist politician.

The UK Independence Party was formed in 1993 with a key policy – to get the UK out of the European Union. With clear, single-issue focus and no-nonsense approach, it has managed to overcome a never-ending string of gaffes and controversies to become part of the political furniture.

The colourful leader loves nothing more than a photo-shoot in the pub, with his gaping mouth breaking into raucous guffawing as he nurses a foaming pint of beer. He may not have swept his party anywhere near Downing Street, but he has tapped into the hearts of a significant proportion of the British electorate.

# What funny weather we've been having!

Floods, storms and waves hit Britain

Once upon a time, wild weather was a rarity in Britain. There was the hurricane of 1987, just before which weatherman Michael Fish famously told BBC viewers not to worry, as there was no such storm on the way. But that was a standout event.

Now, crazy conditions seem to be an annual tradition. The winter of 2010/11 was the coldest since records began, bringing colossal amounts of snow to 'Brrrrritain'. Airports were closed, people died and £13 billion was wiped off the economy. The following summer, the UK was gripped by a heat wave that brought record high temperatures. Then in 2012 and 2013, vast areas of the country suffered record-breaking rainfall and widespread floods.

In the years since, extreme flooding has become commonplace with everywhere from Somerset to Datchet and Cumbria facing biblical deluges during 2014 and 2015. Then came Storm Desmond and Storm Imogen in 2016. You began to wonder why any Brits would be brave enough to leave their homes.

It's long been said British people love to talk about the weather. But most would be happy if such conversations could once again be of the "Isn't it just typical that it rains on Bank Holiday?" variety, rather than "Oh dear, my family are swimming for their lives and my home has floated away."

# Rose garden bromance

Dave and Nick form a coalition government

It started with a (metaphorical) kiss; they never thought it would come to this. They stood side by side in the rose garden, gazing affectionately at one another in the spring sunshine. Over recent weeks they had traded bitter insults but all that was now put to one side as modern Britain's greatest "bromance" got underway.

At the 2010 general election, none of the parties managed the 326 seats needed for an overall majority, so David Cameron and Gordon Brown were forced to desperately scramble around for a coalition partner. Cameron managed to seal a deal, joining forces with Nick Clegg's Liberal Democrats to form a coalition government.

They made for an unlikely duo: each would have to make compromises to get the coalition running, and when previously asked what his favourite political joke was, Cameron had replied: "Nick Clegg".

But as they stood in the Downing Street garden, talking of a "historic and seismic shift" and "new politics", all the background bickering was forgotten. The Dave and Nick show was under way.

# The Annus mirabilis

Britain revels in Her Majesty's jubilee

It may have been a stunt double "Queen Elizabeth" who parachuted into the Olympic Stadium on the opening night of London's Olympic Games, but her Majesty had a remarkable time in 2012.

The Diamond Jubilee, marking the 60th anniversary of her accession to the throne, was celebrated with a series of events including a pageant on the River Thames and a star-studded concert outside Buckingham Palace. There were some hitches: the June weather was positively wintry for a river trip on the royal barge, and Prince Philip missed some of the events with a sudden bladder infection.

But as neighbourhoods around the country partied on the streets, the mood was one of gentle, modern patriotism. The previous year there had been similarly proud revelry when Prince William married Kate Middleton.

When the British public reacted against the Royal Family's perceived stuffiness in the wake of Diana's death in 1997, many would have doubted that the Windsors could ever be so popular again. It had been a right royal bounce-back.

# Brits own the podium

When our athletes went gold

Some people predicted the world would end in 2012. Instead, something even weirder happened – Britain became good at sport.

The first hint that something momentous was in the air came in July, when Andy Murray reached the Wimbledon final, the first Brit to do so for 74 years, and Bradley Wiggins became the first ever British cyclist to win the Tour de France.

Then, at the London Olympic Games, Team GB won 29 gold medals, and 65 medals in total. On one particularly glorious Saturday, the Brits grabbed six golds and one silver.

With the England cricket team's Ashes triumphs in 2009 and 2011 still in the memory, the summer of 2012 almost redefined what it meant to be a British sporting competitor. No longer the foppish, gallant losers, our athletes were now podium-dominating winners. Boy did it feel good, if rather unfamiliar.

Yet one thing stayed the same. Over in Kiev, England's football team crashed out of the European Championship finals after losing a penalty shoot-out.

# Gay weddings and lady bishops

Britain's era of liberal reforms

In the distant eras covered in the earlier pages of this book, such things as same-sex marriage and female bishops would have been simply unthinkable. But in the 21st century, the nation has loosened up and ushered in a wave of liberal reforms.

In 2004, the Civil Partnership act gave same-sex couples the same rights and responsibilities as married heterosexual couples. Then, in 2013, parliament went one step further by legalising same-sex marriage.

Prime minister David Cameron said the move showed Britain's "proud traditions of respect, tolerance and equal worth", but some religious groups were opposed.

The Church of England had its own modernisation going on. Women were permitted to become priests in 1993 but that only opened up the thornier issue of whether women should also be allowed to become bishops. The debate rumbled on until 2012, when female bishops came within a whisker of being approved, before the House of Laity blocked it.

Then, two years later, the General Synod of the Church of England finally allowed women bishops. The landscape of Britain was changing.

# Mad about the boys

One Direction go top of the global pops

During 2010's instalment of ITV talent show *The X Factor*, five young lads were cobbled together into a boy band called One Direction. They went on to conquer the world, spearheading an era of British musical pre-eminence not seen since the swinging sixties.

They were not alone: in the 21st century, British pop stars have been music to the ears of the world, with several UK artists enjoying an era of glorious pop-ularity.

From Amy Winehouse, to Coldplay, Ed Sheeran to Adele, British acts were suddenly shifting phenomenal number of records: one in every seven albums sold globally in 2014 was released by a British artist.

One Direction were the UK's most successful export of the time. They became the first band in the American chart history to have their first four albums debut at number one. Globally, they sold more than 70m records, have achieved more than 100 number ones and performed to more than 10m fans worldwide.

When the band announced a "hiatus" in 2015, teenage girls could be seen weeping across the planet.

# Och aye, or och no?

The Scots vote on independence

Following an agreement between the Scottish and UK governments, Scottish voters are being given the chance to vote on the question: Should Scotland be an independent country?

Please tick one box.

(Result: Nooo: 55.3%, and Aye 44.7%)

# Clarkson clouts a colleague

Top Gear host thumps himself out of a job

In 2015, *Top Gear* presenter Jeremy Clarkson was sacked by the BBC after what the corporation described as an "unprovoked physical attack" on the hit TV show's producer. The assault was said to have been caused because no hot food had been provided by the crew.

Announcing the sacking, the BBC's director general said he recognised it would "divide opinion". Clarkson had been doing just that for years. The colourful character had previously said striking public sector workers should be "shot", he had punched Piers Morgan, and made a number of remarks some people interpreted as racist.

Despite all this, he has built a formidable fan-base. He apologised to the punched producer in 2016. By then, he and his former *Top Gear* sidekicks had found a new home on Amazon streaming television service. With a reported budget for series one of the new venture set at £160 million, Clarkson could have the last laugh – all the way to the bank.

# Jezza defies the odds

Corbyn promises new style of politics

He was supposed to just make up the numbers in an internal party ballot, but instead Jeremy Corbyn might just have ushered in a brand new era for British politics.

Following Labour's defeat at the 2015 general election, party head Ed Miliband stepped down to spend more time with his awkwardness. When the veteran, bearded left-winger Corbyn announced his candidacy for the leadership election, few gave him a chance of finishing anything other than bottom of the pile.

But he only went and won it by a landslide. The jubilant leftie called for a new style of approach to the whole game. "Let us build a kinder politics, a more caring society together," he said. "Let us put our values, the people's values, back into politics."

From the moment he became leader, Corbyn polarised opinion. His supporters welcomed him as an authentic, principled breath of fresh air. His critics mocked him as a poorly dressed, naive and unelectable liability.

Whether he will indeed change the landscape of British politics remains to be seen. But, regardless of political affiliation, many Brits couldn't help but admire this Great British underdog for the way he got to the top table. But could he go on to change the face of Britain?

# A Brit of all right!

We're ruddy brilliant, we are!

From the Farmer Giles of the Neolithic Age to 21st-century Britain, we've taken you through the story so far of these fine isles. Along the way, there have been triumphs and failures, comedy and bloodshed, plus tales of courage, endeavour and eccentricity. Oh, and a few cups of tea, too. So settle down with a cuppa and savour the climax of the story.

In November 2003, the English rugby team walked in Captain Cook's footsteps to Australia and returned with the World Cup trophy. Victory was assured with a drop goal just 26 seconds from the end by Jonny Wilkinson. England had actually won a sporting trophy for a change! No wonder we lined the streets of London to welcome them home.

Following the terrific triumphs of 2012, Brits are continuing to succeed in sport, proving that the Olympic year was not a flash in the pan. Andy Murray became the first man from Great Britain to win the Wimbledon singles title since Fred Perry in 1936, England's cricketers won the Ashes in 2013 and 2015, and Bradley Wiggins has added new honours to his list. Cue repeated celebrations among British fans of all religions and races.

We Brits have not always been quick to unite and celebrate our great nation, but we're getting better at it. Here's to many more excuses to wave the Union Flag with pride in future. Cheers!

# Other titles in this series include:

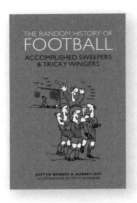

ISBN 978-1-85375-936-9

ISBN 978-1-85375-940-6

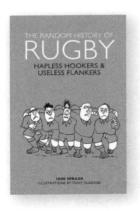

ISBN 978-1-85375-939-0

ISBN 978-1-85375-938-3